Barearse Boy

Barearse Boy
Jon Tait

Smokestack Books
1 Lake Terrace, Grewelthorpe, Ripon HG4 3BU
e-mail: info@smokestack-books.co.uk
www.smokestack-books.co.uk

Barearse Boy
Copyright 2015, Jon Tait, all rights reserved.

ISBN 978-0-9929581-9-0

Smokestack Books is represented by Inpress Ltd

for Sally

Contents

Kinmont's Bairns	11
Big Meeting	12
Saturday	13
State of Play	15
Striker	16
Border – A Family History in Two Parts	17
Conti's	18
The Dressing Room	19
8 'til 8	20
Muckle Mooth Meg	21
Demolition	22
Scar Tissue	23
0-4	24
Turnbull's Dog	25
Ghost Shirt	26
Pub Story	27
Velocity	28
Laying Floorboards	30
Nicked	31
New Boots	32
Goodbye Pork Pie Hat	34
Leek Show	35
County Cup Tie	36
Poacher's Pocket	37
Dorty Get	38
Retrospective	39
Evil Eye	40
The River	41
Coast	42
Any Port in a Storm	43
London	44
A Friend of Mine	45
Bullet Holes	46
Chief	47
Fortune Teller	48
The A-Team	49

Doors Day	50
New Astronauts	51
Night-time Street Brawl	52
Cup Final	53
Bottles	54
We Are	55
One Big Win	56
End of the Night	57
Cold Steel Trigger	58
Childhood	59
Tartans Flapping	60
School	61
I Believe	62
Sermon	64
In B/W	65
Broken Spectre	66
Phase 4	67
Granny Glasses	68
Birthday Balloons	69
15 Miles	70
Red Fist	71
Blood Kit	72
Circus	74
Night Shift	75
Home	76
Border Reiver	77
One More Tab	78
Journey into Space	79
Pigeon	80
Two Steps Back	81
For Real	82
Pedal Power	83
Playing with Snakes	84
Family Tree	85
March or Die	86
Dirty Jobs	87
Haunted	88
Boom of the Bass	89

Regrets	90
Cosmic Gratitude	91
Haircut	92
Picket Line	93
Hillside	94
The Egg Shack	95
Bitter End	96
Comparing Tattoos	97
Dawn	98
The Girl from the Scree Hills & the Girl from the Red City	99
I Can Tell You the Names	103
Dark Country Night	104
Lost	105
We Are Hill People	106
Red	108
Grain	110
Sick	111
Just like Oz	112
Thunderflash	113
Railroad	114
Warning	115
Starlings	116
Fate	117
Hot Trod	119
Full Moon	120
Best Get Drunk	121
The Glory of War	122
The Darkness	123

Kinmont's Bairns

There's a mosaic of the capture of Kinmont Willie
on the underpass wall.
Bearded, defiant, trussed up on horseback
with a cheering crowd following behind.
Funny, but they don't have one
of his escape from the square red fortress.

No-one scrawls graffiti on this wall,
as if his power and influence have carried on
down the centuries when now
he'd be sitting in a back room of a barbers,
a butcher shop or bookies
hair starting to go bald at the crown
open-collared polo shirt
the flash of gold from his thick chain
against his hairy chest, holding court
like Tony Soprano,
hot espresso and cigarettes on his breath
with his crew sat around like crocodiles.

We're all Kinmont's bairns now.

Big Meeting

Packed into the hall with red lodge banner
loud jabbering voices of angry conversations, confusion,
screeching chairs, men in black donkey jackets
with orange back panels
smoke drifting and clinging in yellow, grey and brown clouds
we'd seen the scabs bussed into the pit
with mesh on the windows like Belfast
then the union man with large sideburns
brylcreemed hair and crumpled white shirt
tucked unevenly into a baggy suit
stands at the front with arms raised
as the commotion dies down and says
Wuh've browt yuh ahl here tuh let yuh knaa
whaat wuh knaa, lads.

A short pause, expectation.

Wuh knaa nowt.

Back to the pickets, the Russian food parcels.

Saturday

The seagulls lined up
on the back breeze block wall
shriek mockery at the goalkeeper
with bobbing heads.

Large empty skies
grey as old chewing gum
as the fog steadily lifts,
revealing the red, white & blue
of Union Jack flags
hanging limply from
the green perimeter fence.

Shadowy ghosts hidden
behind the nicotine-yellow net curtains
of crumbling bacon & egg B&Bs
with sauce clagged round the bottle top
the bookies & pubs
& cheap discount stores

those lost names a muster call
howked out of the black belly
of the earth
& trundled along the belt…

Bates
Ellington
Whittle

programme folded in jeans back pocket,
groundsman poking a fork in the pitch.

The music from the p.a. speakers
distant, gone in the wind,
blown out of the ground with
swirling empty crisp packets.

Corner flags flapping
like Tibetan prayer silks.

State of Play

The game belongs behind rows
of neat allotments & red brick terraces & pigeon duckets
watched by gadgies in flat caps
called norman & ted & frank
coughing coal dust into white hankies
in a stand that looks like an old cow hemmel
with the ripe stench of boiling onions & pies
& chip fat cutting the cold air
while a red glow from the steel works
illuminates the grey afternoon skies
as rain falls heavy as black bullets
from the gathering gloom
stotting off corrugated tin sheets
rather than in soulless concrete coliseums
where the flat warm beer in plastic cups
costs an hour's wages
& they've never heard of ham & pease pudding stotties.

Striker

The sharp metal chink of trowel on brick
deftly slapping down a new course of grey compo
scraped from a plastic bucket by
those lime-calloused fingers that
could also unsnap a bra in one swift move
& you'd never have thought
that a man in blue overalls with such quick hands
could also have such skilful feet
with a white ball on the green turf.

A brief rumble of approval
a yellow Metro train passing through
an underground station
as the ball crashes into the roof of the net
like discarded trawlermen's lobster pots
on the harbour at Seahouses
& shakes the rainwater free with a dull swish.

Border – A Family History in Two Parts

1513

That bloody Willie Turnbull nicked my fucking horse. Can you believe it? Right there in the middle of the fucking carnage with arrows thumping into flesh & tangling with billhooks, slipping in the mud and blood, colourful banners crushed into the sodden earth, the lion not-so-fucking rampant & Turnbull does off with my grey mare. The fly bastard. I lift my helmet, sweat stinging my eyes, face flecked red from swinging my sword at Englishmen & my fucking horse is gone. I'm off to see the King. What's that? He's dead too? Oh, for fuck's sake. Who's in charge then? I want my fucking horse back, pronto.

1603

Union of the Crowns? You fucking what? Five years I've spent in dingy, dark stone cells with heavy chains on my skin in the company of men like Sim Armstrong of Whitehaugh & some of the roughest characters on the whole fucking Border, man. Sure, we jumped the walls at York, so close to the river I could taste the moisture in the night air but now I've been ill with the ague and dropsy, sweating in a fucking peat hole, hallucinating and fevered & three fucking grand it's cost me for the privilege, then you tell me that England's got a Scottish King? So can I fucking go home now? I need to feel the splash of the cold Stank on my face. Get me back to Town Yetholm. Back to the rounded green Cheviot hills. Just get me back home.

Conti's

bruno conti's uncle
had a chippy
in amble.

mediterranean moustache
smart white coat
& folded arms

as the cod
straight off the grey north sea
sizzled in batter

like the ticker-tape
reception for the azzuri
or the distant commentary

from the T.V. set
in the front room
donned in 70s wallpaper

silent pride wrong side of hadrian's frontier
the bright trawlers are tethered to the harbour walls
the pit head wheels are in museums.

The Dressing Room

Sharp clack of studs on the cold concrete floor
like pit ponies hooves in the darkness,
the smell of deep heat & stale hops & sweat
rolls of bandages & black insulating tape,
the silky touch of a shirt pulled from the kit bag
with it's guts spilled open in the middle of the floor
I'll only wear 3 or 7 or 10, gaffer;
little superstitious rituals, the lucky Y-fronts,
watches & rings collected in the manager's pocket
& he says Get tight to ya man, get stuck in from the off,
Divn't dee nowt fancy, Get it up the park;
Nervous laughter, nodding, & the clapping of hands
as the door swings open
& we jog onto the turf
with stomachs doing little flips.

8 'til 8

My mate Mickey's first motor was a beat-up two-tone chocolate brown 1970s Marina & we had to stuff the headlights with loft insulation as they splayed out at weird angles so the road ahead wasn't lit up too well but you could see what was in the hedgerows alongside just fine so we pull up outside a Rave December 1992 cold fresh moonlit night with frost on the road industrial south east Northumberland slag heaps & pit wheels gone replaced with Japanese electrical components factories when a lass in silver hot pants & roller boots & glitter eye shadow dishing out flyers taps on the passenger window to hand me one & I have to shrug and hold out my hands as I can't roll the window down as we'd had to wedge it up in place with old clothes pegs jammed in the bottom we certainly knew how to travel in style wearing black leather coats & jeans & designer T-shirts with rubber sleeves & black pants with silver pocket zips & boots for stomping 12 hours straight with sweat pouring the dull throb of the basslines vibrating through the car above the purring engine face flushing red coming up on E & the anticipation that this could be the greatest night of your life.

Muckle Mooth Meg

She's not that bad when you get a good look at her, man.
Her pretty blue eyes that I'd never have noticed
And never mind her huge gob, it's always set in a wide smile.
Amazing how attractive a pair of tits can become
When a rope around the neck is your other option.

Aye, I know I said it was nowt for a Scott to die,
Full of piss and vinegar bravado,
But I'd rather be stiff in a bed with muckle mooth Meg
Than hanging stiff from a tree.

Demolition

They knocked down
my nana's raa
when they built
the slip-road past the ground.

Old yellowing sports pages
pasted on blue walls,
club crest, grainy goal celebrations
programme covers & tickets.

The dog track around the pitch crumbling,
memories of '50s advertisements
on gable ends, men in suits
smelling of aftershave & brylcreem
on a night out at the pictures.

Mug of coffee in Mario's café,
watching housewives in jeans & leather jackets
weighed down with plastic shopping bags
walking past a hero cast in bronze
belting an invisible ball perpetually
up a red pedestrianised street.

A pounding drum rattling
round the high, dark rafters
like a defiant heartbeat
while councillors in cheap pinstripes
want to flatten the lot
& build supermarkets.

Scar Tissue

This town's full of knuckle-nose hardmen squeezed into leather jackets, necks like bulls, tougher than a shipyard rivet. rainwater on shaved heads like velcro, running boxing clubs & protection rackets & drug rings & post office raids from streets slanting down towards the river full of curved bridges & though you hear stories of sawn-off shotguns & petrol cans & plyers they love nowt better than a fist fight, the smack of bone on bone, standing scowling on red brick terrace corners with pit-bull terriers & glue-sniffing foot soldiers in kappa tracksuits on bmx bikes while cctv cameras on lampposts whir into action & cars full of joyriders & ramraiders cruise up & down the streets of asian newsagents & bookies & boarded-up travel agents & you'll be lucky to get a job & the cancer or a heart attack will kill you in your 50s & the kitchens smell of stale chip fat & the jagged white scar of old stitches runs like a relief map of the coast down your cheek but it's still home & your chest puffs out like a pigeon each time the high rises & the civic centre seahorses profile against the sky, grey as pavements & flat as a plate.

0-4

Hands on hips
heads bent low
as early daffodils drenched in rain
the keeper sits in a pool of mud
with a look of disgruntlement etched
on his face & the ball nestled
in the net behind him
& you don't know whether to laugh
or cry
or boot the goalpost.

Turnbull's Dog

at Halidon Hill

It's mair than just a feeling of unease;
the dreek day draining energy flat.
Steady light patter on the brown earth
churned over soft and pliable
sated by the blood of men
haunted by a black vibration of defeat.
The sense of invisible eyes watching on,
a silent spectral army,
hair matted and flattened by rain
tartans torn and flapping forlorn
the big dark mastiff loyal, awaiting,
heeled by the giant Scottish champion,
guarding his spot, his ghostly history,
mournful features fading into the mist,
sad pipes distant, misheard in the wind,
Berwick's red rooftops bright by the sea.

Ghost Shirt

The heavy leather jacket
Creaks as I breath.

This is a strange island;
They sell us lighters & trinkets
w/ dancing devils emblazoned
At the local hippy market stalls.

I wrap an Aztec poncho around my head,
The rolling sweat stinging my eyes,
A giant Smiley logo blazing down.
Oh, but you cannot see me
Hidden in these hills;
Tramping up thru red dust
In lizard-skin fellahin boots,
An infinity snake tattoo
Blue on my burned arm
Like a crumpled five pound note.
The debris of Techno.

I moved w/ a dark girl
invisible in volcanic valleys,
Her hips were smooth
As a VW beetle
& hot.

Bez directed the dance,
Wading thru treacle
On doves.

Pub Story

Auld Jack played oot on the wing
fought in the International Brigades
in Spain
& got a limp in Ebro
yellow dust powdered face
dull metal clang of a bullet
punching into a steel helmet
he copped a shard of shrapnel
for the cause
& married a Spanish lass
that he met in the hospital
who scrubbed the soot
off their red terrace step
& instead of olive trees saw
smoke billowing out of chimney stacks
a wet gleam like calm seas on the roof slates
shipyard cranes peering out of the gloom
& do you knaa, bonny lad,
he couldn't half cross a bahl.

Velocity

Pink, hot & scaled like a snake's back
the faint blue of a fading sailor's swallow tattoo
on cream rubber
down like burst pillows & dust
slowly spinning like a galaxy in a shaft of sunlight.

The bare boards slippery with muck
scraped up with an old coal shovel
& hurled on the leek trench
glinting greens and purples and blues
on a long slender neck
with watchful orange eye betraying lizard ancestry
scanning over the dark shapes of hills

the frantic surge of volcanic rock
forced up through the crust and cooled
then carved by the ice and wind over millennia.

A whole history in red leather bound
Up North Combine books on a shelf
behind a sagging old sofa seat
& the Ceylon tea chests stamped with arcane lettering
on thin balsa wood & filled with beans
like polished balls of bark.

BLUE CHEQUERED HEN 3275
MEALY COCK 2963

in steady blocked blue biro.
Three plastic nesting eggs
a brittle, yellowed copy of the Daily Mirror
& a paint-splattered work radio
the grey metallic clock's steady tick
& a soft coo from the boxes.

Paired a tumbler with a tumbler
& saw the green earth racing up
to meet the spinning fall
at velocity.

Laying Floorboards

Jogged over to take a corner
& joked to the linesman
I'm ganna bend this into the top corner, man
floated in over the keeper's head
hit the metal stanchion at the back post
& walked back laughing.

I'm a trainee joiner on £135 a week
3 hours ago I was laying floor boards.

Nicked

We were drunk & decided to kidnap a mate from his girlfriend's apartment for a laugh & as we went up the dark night street giggling with tan nylons tight over our faces a police car pulled up in a flash of blue revolving lights & when the cops asked us what we were doing, what could we say but shrug & mumble through the stockings, noses squashed flat, hands held high, the jumbled sound of voices crackling over the radio.

New Boots

They must have been constructed
in some grey state-owned factory
like Ladas & Trabants
& they didn't go down well
with the lads in the changing rooms
when edged gingerly out of the school bag.

The region gripped by unemployment
& the miner's strike

Even men in orange flashed donkey jackets
grinned at the sight
of my new black Bokta boots
that my fathaa got cheap
as they'd been in the shop window
for months.

paint splattered bib & brace
grey stubble & the glowing dog end
of a Regal ordinary
hot as his temper.

They'll be fine, man

But even I got a laugh
when Mickey's mam got him a pair
of Bobby Charlton specials from the charity shop

all dull brown leather
like building site steel toe-cappers
that smashed the solid old white Mitre multiplex
& didn't hurt his feet at all

Then lay hidden in the back of the shed
behind the humming large white freezer
so as not to hurt her feelings

while some kid in Puma 'Maradona Kings'
couldn't even make the team.

Goodbye Pork Pie Hat

Uncle graham always had a great knack for nicknames; the chinaman, mucky mick, johnny three-spins the barber, camouflage scotty who donned a paras crap hat & went off to join the raf regiment, ninja dave & thistle bush who ordered full black kit through the royal mail & we laughed as they crawled up the grass hill at the back of the estate, waiting for them to spin themselves into the ground or out of a tree in a shower of copper leaves, a blue swallow tattoo from a youthful seaside drinking trip high on his powerful arm as he hammered nails into a roof with a heavy, steady rap, or supped the foaming top off a pint of best scotch in the railway, recalling with a hand over his mouth & glint in his eye the three-tiered dog turd he dubbed the coiled cobra of coplish & the building site poetry 'goodbye, pork pie hat' & 'singing songs to my member,' each word as carefully crafted as his mortice & tenon joints that slipped together smoothly in the dusty joiners shop.

Leek Show

Men clean the white beards
and slender green leaves
on three fine vegetables
at the social club leek show -
First prize a week in Tenerife.

While a biker with 13 tattooed on his forehead
borstal dots on his knuckles
stands at the bar in greasy jeans
denim jacket with the sleeves cut off
 & heavy metal T-shirt
telling bullshit Barlinnie jail stories.

Get us drunk, corrallino,
lead us blinking into the sunlight
of tyneside's soot-blackened back streets
from the bowels of a bustling boozer.
No picturesque red pan tiled roofs
on pastel coloured buildings here
No olive trees, no bowl of cacciuco at a port café.

Just an ugly green riveted bridge
railway sidings & 1950s scrapyard adverts
on disused red brick warehouse gables.

The ghosts of the Jarrow marchers
faded black & white in cloth caps
ribs showing like a whippets
crowd in high narrow alleys as we lurch out

through the sturdy wooden door
a trawler on the swell
guided by a neon blue star.

County Cup Tie

Rusty orange & red wings of the Gateshead Angel
like the pitted side of a bent Vauxhall Astra
in some forgotten corner of a scrap yard.

Lost among the pylons,
old shunters in railway sidings,
huge round gas cylinders &
portakabins of an industrial estate.

Loose hanging white goal nets
from metal goal frames
hung off a bar stool,
black clarts heavy with river silt
in the worn goalmouth.
Pools of water in the dipped white lime lines.

After, the steady thump of darts
pounding the board
& a rap of dominoes
tapping the table top
in the Welfare Club.
Foamy tops of pints ruby in the glass.

Orange & white neon street lights
Shimmering across the inky black Tyne.

Poacher's Pocket

Crunching slowly through brittle frosted grass
with breath pulled tight in the lungs,
the moon peering through gnarled tree branches
& glinting icicles thicker than a finger
while the green waxed jacket snaps like a sail.

My father, hair golden & curly as Roger Daltry,
slipped the cleek from his coat sleeve
& bent by a black pool with ice
sculpted into shapes sleek as glass
with the rush of the river in his ears like guitar static.

He saw Hendrix and The Who
at the Isle of Wight festival
in flared jeans & black cowboy boots & red t-shirt tan
& when I ask him how far has was from the stage
he jokes 'aboot Birkenhead.'

It was a winter of power cuts, blackouts,
of orange candlelight flickering long shadows
up bare woodchip walls in thick silence
& my father made his way home through the darkness,
the dead weight of a gaffed trout in his poacher's pocket
thumping his ribs in the regular rhythm of his stride.

Dorty Get

He's a dorty get, man
grabs your shirt at corners
tramples on your toes
flicks your feet away when the ref's not looking
jumps with his elbows leading
arms blue as fivers with tattoos
shaven head & old white scars

Even the lass in the Comrades Club
called him a dorty get
when he made a lunge at her assets
between the optics
& bad renditions of Elvis.

Oh, aye, he's still the skipper, like.
He might be a dorty get,
but he's our dorty get.

Whey, you wouldn't want to play against him, man.

Retrospective

My Granda
Shelled the Jap army
In Burma.

Wet & humid
Under the dense, green
Dark canopy of leaves.
Foisty smell of jungle decay.

Mist shrouded the green hills
In washy watercolours.
Guns boomed around the valley like thunder.

Me?
I stand in the steaming street
Backed by black volcanic mountains
In flip-flops & khaki shorts
Hurling beer glasses & plastic chairs
At the baton-wielding police,
Dodging the wild white burst
Of a water cannon.

Evil Eye

The goalkeeper has an evil eye
penned in black marker
on the palm of his hand
hidden by the soft fabric of his gloves,
fiddling with the Velcro
on his wrist straps at a corner
shouting instructions, pointing,
feeling his fingers stretched
as he hurls his head back,
tips the ball over the bar
to groans from the opposition
& lands on the turf
with a dull, heavy slap,
the smell of wet grass & soil
filling his head.

He'll be back on site in the morning,
palms scrubbed clean with a brillo pad,
stale sweat from his gloves still lingering
like hotching egg butties in a plastic bait box.

The River

It must have been some sight – the bustle on Tyne Dock as crates of Ceylon tea swang down in great nets from grimy freighters, proud men, a few bob & a red Party card in a brown leather wallet worn smooth as a pilot's bomber jacket fat in the double-breasted black coat, hands calloused as old oak bark, with the rising gabble of foreign voices in busy warehouses, the slick on the dark river gleaming like a rainbow & smoke billowing out of stacks over the green arch of the bridge, nine thousand in flat caps packed under the rusting corrugated roof at Redheugh to watch Gateshead in the League, walking whippets down the back rows of red brick terraces with outdoor netties, but now the flour mills' an art gallery, the neon quayside bustles with stag & hen parties, all pink feather boas & plastic L plates, staggering into the road pissed on cheap alcopops, the whirr of engines & machinery replaced by the dull thump of Euro Techno, Broon Ale replaced by Chardonnay.

Coast

Goalnets rolled out of the dark innards
of an upturned wooden fishing boat
with doors in the stern like a hut,
as long grasses sway with a steady swish
on top of sand dunes by lonely sentries
of old World War Two pill boxes,
players calls filling the large blue sky
broken by castles on the horizon;
smoking kippers in an old stone building
in the tight narrow streets of a
fishing village sloping down
to the empty long beaches of
driftwood, orange rope, shells,
crabs in rock pools & the
white breakers low roar rolling in
off the grey North Sea,
a bracing wind wobbling the ball
in the air like an egg
as we play the sons of our fathers opponents
from old black & white team snapshots
the sideburns, moustaches, beards & long hair
like a 60s rock band on tour are gone
but the names remain the same,
the sad eerie moan of a foghorn
ticking off the generations
steady as a metronome.

Any Port in a Storm

If aa'd been a manashee they'd have called me Trieste, the legacy of some distant sailing gadgie in the family, howking the canvass kit bag ower the shoulder of his thick grimy white wool jumper & tipping his black maritime hat at a jaunty angle, hauling ropes on wooden decks slippery wi fish guts & oil though hands coarse as clemmies that would click as they ran up the warm stockings of a open-legged mott with hair dark as a craa's wing, salt thick in the stubble as he licked his lips in anticipation, filling his gob wi peeve like rum & broon ale in some rough dockside bar wi sawdust on the floor. Cursing some gowk in the wheelhoose as the white waves crashed over the hull & watching on from a porthole squeaky wi condensation as the ship tethered up in San Francisco or Naples or Tangiers, smoke billowing from the stacks & the sad horn announcing their arrival, & every tattoo would tell a story – the swallows & nautical star for home, a pig & a rooster, Aye, he'd see fun fairs on shore leave, the world's strongest man with waxed moustache & leopard skin, bearded ladies & strange foetuses in glass bottles then clash on for kelter in the sweating metal riveted womb, strange notes rolled up in his pocket & fanned oot in the hammock then hidden in an auld baccy tin with his memories, his dreams.

London

We drove a Landrover down to Tilbury Docks
For a dodgy local garage owner
To ship out to South Africa
& the bloke in a uniform said:
Just save us the time & tell us where the gear is, lads
So we had to sit in a Portakabin
As they took the vehicle apart
Then they made us walk miles
Back to the train station when they found nowt
& then as we sat on the grass
In a central London park
The Special Branch pulled us
Because some nosy fucker misheard our accents,
Thought the trade plates were Irish,
& reckoned we were the IRA,
Then the only kindness we received
Was when an elderly Italian mamma
In a sandwich shop cried – You're-a Geordies!
& wouldn't take our money, cradling the cash
Closed in our palms like the trembling, warm feathers
Of an injured bird, & gave us extra butties & a warm smile
But you can't get Regal ordinary cigarettes
The beer's weak as piss
& the women cut you down with an icy glare
So it was with a sense of relief
That we boarded the National Express back up north,
Cradling our cans & hoping to make last orders
As we sped up the motorway,
Green road signs flashing past the window.

A Friend of Mine

A friend of mine
An ex-monk
Ex-publican
Ex-fish and rice proprietor
w/ an extraordinary rich English accent
& a Sri-Lankan wife
Wants me to join his expedition
w/ some other lads from the pub
To retrieve the Holy Grail.
'I know where it is,' he says
'Ethiopia. One guard on the entrance.
We rollup in an armoured car,
Do WHATEVER IS NECCESARY
To remove the guard
& get the bugger out.'

The sand is my sleeping bag

Let's Go.

Bullet Holes

Marija the serbian barmaid wanted to work in london
& was duped by some agency
into this dark corner of northumberland
enveloped in hills & sky black as new bruises
& she looks like rosalba neri
sultry beauty of 70s cinema
so i raise a glass of sambuca
to her eyes all black olive & cappuccino
& smoking like mt. etna
as she sings us a schooldays song to tito
& confides to me conspiratorially
that she wants to become a spy,
conjuring images trench coats & ladas, barbed wire,
whispered messages & codes,
but still i cannot see the bombing raids
the twisted metal & bullet holes in her smile.

Chief

The old Indian Chief
wears cowboy boots & jeans
& a brown suede jacket
with full feather head dress
& when he tells you to
'Keep in the wind'
I think of the wild geese
of your Irish heritage.
There are Aztec spiders & monkeys
on the cloth over the speaker,
the rattle of shells
& you are blessed by a shamanic chant
outside a shopping centre
that you may never remember.
But I will.

Fortune Teller

Blue & white striped shirts
hang neatly off pegs
with seahorse badge & numbers
obscured in the folds of material,
shorts & socks folded smartly
on the wooden benches
of the silent changing rooms
heavy with pregnant expectation.

All those childhood memories
of the white dome at Spanish City,
metallic laughter & space invaders
the schoolyard chaos of a penny arcade,
of slot machines, dodgems & wheels,
the clatter of coins from a tuppence shuffler.
Ice cream cone from Arrighi's
melting fast in the oppressive heat,
the sticky sweet white lines
running down the back of an arm
& dripping off the elbow
red with sun burn.

& all those nights
with wild women under a blue neon star
thronging busy chatter in a packed pub,
the low thump of the bass through a toilet door
then picking up kebabs from the Tasty Turks
before waking on some strange settee
& looking out of a large bay window
scanning the horizon beyond St. Mary's lighthouse
for Viking longboats
or irate husbands.

The fortune teller wore a red paisley shawl.
Crossed her palms with silver
& she foresaw the Twin Towers of Wembley
in the mists of the crystal ball.

The A-Team

I'm waiting to splurge some brown sauce
on a piping hot haggis & tattie pie
by the hatch of the refreshment hut at Galabank
when the A-Team theme tune
blares out of the speakers
on the end of the small tidy stand
with the club's name picked out in black & yellow seats
& the players run out onto the pitch
from the red brick clubhouse,
but there's no B.A. Barracus in the squad.

No Evel Knievel. No stars & stripes.
A patchwork quilt of St. Andrew's crosses
hang from the gable end of the bar,
sticky with Tennent's Lager like honey.

Doors Day

The times when the rising skeleton of a ship's hull could blot out the sunlight at the end of a terrace & the dull clank of rivets on steel punctuated the day & you could set your watch by the bustle of men on shift change at the yard gates have been consigned to old newsreels & as we don't want to fry thin chips in a fast-food restaurant or wipe backsides in a care home we've got nowt better to do than shuffle our feet & cough dryly, nicotine in our lungs rather than industrial dust, with an expectant clink of bottles in co-op bags at a council flat door on easter sunday morning for our annual doors day celebration as inside shoes slides a vinyl record carefully from its sleeve & as it slowly revolves with a prickly pick-up on the deck we begin ripping the tops off cans & jim morrison's voice booms clear & loud from the speakers intoning a prayer embraced by a generation of men raised by women & without heavy manual labour so a heavy fog of cannabis smoke has enveloped the room by the time we've had the soft parade & we're bouncing off the walls after l.a. woman as shoes places the records back in a careful stack & we're ready to stumble pissed into the pub next door shouting pretty neat, far gone getting up close to the firm curved arse of a lass at the bar, breath heavy with hops & red-eyed, quoting poems & lyrics & knocking over bar-stools but this isn't california & it isn't the 1960s & maybe we would have never gone into the shipyards or the pits anyway & just maybe we were always too much for this town & the search for some mystic illumination goes on & the only way we'll break on thru to the other side is by kicking the fucking windows in.

New Astronauts

We are the new astronauts
& this is our time.

I kissed her leather-clad thighs
& the tears welled up
deep in my eyes.

Eve of breakdown

Strange mountains

Hurry! bolt the doors
& hide the insane sun.
Our time is coming to an end.

Night-time Street Brawl

A large purple sky
& a hot breeze blowing in
From Africa.
Sipping lager on the veranda
Dreaming of cunts
& the inside of sea shells.

A sudden dull electric rumble
Rises above the booming basslines
Which drift up from the clubs.
I an enthralled;
Is it a riot,
Or an armed uprising?

The flashing blue lights
Of a Police van
Revolving in the shop fronts.
A mad smash of bottles
& lads in Man. City shirts
Storming down a neon street
Then retreating like the tide.

I need a pistol
Or a sawn-off shotgun
To fire into the heavy air.

I am the Sundance kid.

Cup Final

People in T-shirts with red forearms standing with pints
on the small terrace steps by the reflected glass
of the clubhouse bar, emptied for the presentation,
low summer evening sun casting long shadows
over the pitch while a grey haired auld fella
from the FA stands at a table on the touchline
talking in monotone for what seems ages
then a cheer and sudden applause
like the clatter of a startled pigeon's wings
from the tight three-deep semi-circle
of fans, young kids & wives
& you're holding your boots between two fingers,
socks rolled down to the ankles,
joking with a gang of lads in baseball caps
taking a swig from a can of Tartan Bitter
to get a laugh & they're patting your back
as you shuffle to the end of a line of team-mates
walking forward slowly to cheers
& shaking hands with the FA man,
opponents slouched on the turf clapping
some on honkers with shirts hung over bare shoulders
when a sudden rush of horror sweeps over you
as you glance at the pile of velvet boxes on the table
& quickly calculate that there aren't enough medals to go round
so when you're finally there at the table for your moment
you don't get a handshake or nowt else
& subs are opening their boxes for a look
then quickly hiding them in tracksuit pockets
& there's no chance they'll give one up for you
so you shake your head slowly & walk away
embarrassed & bitter, isolated & angry,
hiding your emotions with a gag,
asking a peroxide blonde with fake tan for a bottle of lager
& pretending you're not bothered,
thinking 'Keep your bloody Champagne.
I hope it chokes you.'

Bottles

Drinking bottled Irish anger
From the streams of pain
In the North.

Losing control
Eyes starting to roll
Fell off the bar stool.

We're dancing on an icy ledge
With fire in our eyes.

We Are

We are the Votadini
Scourge of Rome
Faces brown with dried blood
& war paint, wild matted hair.
Hard as the barren heather hills
Pissing on the broken bodies of centurions.

There are no mosaics
This side of the wall
No fabulous columns, no luxurious baths.

We do not recognise your Imperial Eagle
Peaty whisky fumes on our breath
Screaming down out of scree slopes
Like the high call of the curlew.

Though they call this green island
The United Kingdom,
We remain the Votadini,
Proud in the mists & the moors.

We are what awaits you
At the edge of the world.

One Big Win

I was just a kid the first time I walked into a bookies sent in to look for an old relative The Sheriff a notorious womaniser & poacher all flat caps & jackets & woodbine smoke but that same reek of desperation still clings like a body bag the slowly torn slips fit for the church steps at a wedding showering the wooden floor smoother than an old bar top as a big treble goes down by a nose to a 33-1 shot & though you know the sport's fixed you still crave that rush the colourful silks & sturdy animals gleaming sheen in the sun with hooves tearing up the turf like dull thunder & you start ignoring the form & looking for mystical tips some crazy hunch on the names that's maybe given by an angel or even a devil who cares as long as it romps home & you still end up chasing your tail like a handsome black cat in an empty bath hoping & lusting for that one big win like a junkie needs the jag of the needle & sweating as the small irate Chinese man starts jabbering angrily under the sick yellow light in the back street gambling den & brothel & you wonder if he has a pistol or meat cleaver hidden under the bar as you slap down a pile of purple notes drink up & get out into an alley where the neon lights glimmer on the pavement like the sea.

End of the Night

Long, entwined, majestic hair
And softly scented whiskey breath.

Quiet, crisp, black leather
Lizard-skin clothes.
A piercing, doomed scream
Could summon the dead.

Would you be a satyr
And follow me to enlightenment?

Idols on the eve of destruction.
The flower doomed by the power
Of money.

Listen…
Her pussy was a warm, wet cave
Under patient exploration;
Even as he breathed he fell,
Riding his panther through
Pools of blood and water.

Cold Steel Trigger

Coming back from the Reading Festival a homeless guy in a train station is about to hit us for some cash until he sees our pile of old green canvass kit bags & says Are you lads in the Army? though who knows what freakish unit he thinks we are in as we stand around smoking & swigging from cans in jeans & boots & leather jackets all stubble & scowls from lack of sleep & although we say no & offer him some change he won't take it & slinks off disturbed in the misapprehension that Her Majesty's Armed Forces contains a regiment of blokes as wild-looking as Apocalypse Now picturing us hanging out the back of a helicopter with a Gatling gun rattling brass cases flying out & The Doors booming from a tape deck as the jungle below burns with fingers on a cold steel trigger rather than slipping inside the warm hot-pants & nylon tights of grunge chicks in knee-high boots & the thrill of feeling the soft but firm curls of pubic hair & silky wet slip of moist pink lips as she sighs softly with clammy breath panting on the nape of your neck.

Childhood

Snotty nose wiped on the back sleeve
of a woolly jumper with big snowflakes on the front
brown cords, blonde hair sticking up straight out of bed
when a neighbour on the pre-fab estate
all pebbled-dashed with car engines in the overgrown grass
broken wooden front fences & skateboards
bikes and house bricks scattered on the road
kids pictures in chalk on the pavement
caught me at the bottom of their garden
with their pet tortoise raised to my gob
& when she asked what I was doing
I replied excitedly that I'd found a pie with legs.

Tartans Flapping

We're watching the build up to the big fight on the TV screens in the Sports Bar Puerto Del Carmen with the walls covered in framed signed photographs of stars & a load of sunburned skinhead tattooed cockneys & brummies sat on the bar stools & when big Stevie Collins looms up on the screens bouncing up to the ring Sky Sports start playing bagpipes & showing wide panoramic shots of green hills & purple heather & trees & we're instantly feeling homesick after spending our time in the bleak burnt red & orange & black volcanic landscape with little shrubs & olive bushes & wide quiet roads with small white kerbstones & low cool lava walls & the relentless sun feeling nostalgic for the rain & fog & the smell of wet bracken & the skirling pipes start my blood pumping betraying my true heritage as a Town Yetholm laird & Mickey is transported back to Glencoe half covered in heavy raincloud & Paul is cleaning glasses behind the bar with a mad glint in his eyes like Highlander as the cockneys start booing & all our genes are bouncing & heads spinning from too much cheap cold lager adrenalin & 400 years of battle as we prepare to go to war with tartans flapping around our knees.

School

They don't bandy about words like poverty of deprivation
when half the shaven-headed class is on free dinner chitties
for state supported chips & beans
& the knees of your black pants are slick from wear
& when you slap a lad on the back in the dinner hall
a load of cutlery lifted for home crashes on the floor
leaving him beaming red like a lighthouse beacon
but we're no longer washing in a tin bath by a coal fire
or pissing in an outside brick netty
so everything must be alright then
& though we don't have much money
we have fists & foreheads & feet & flashing tempers
& segs in the soles of our shoes
& when some mean-faced fucker in a suit
questions your qualifications in an interview
you grab him by the tie & smash his chin off the desk
& walk out the door laughing thinking fuck it
fuck it all.

I Believe

I'd like to sit & smoke a cigarette, sip at a cappuccino from a white mug at a french café table with a bearded eric cantona looking cool in his dark glasses & brown suede jacket listening to jazz & blues & i'd tell him how much i admire his disdain for authority & how he played the game like it should be played with a swagger, a glint in the eye, collar turned up, looking down a long nose at little men in black uniforms brandishing cards who can't comprehend the imagination & i'd like to shake george best's hand & tell him you were right to pretend to swig from those empty cans chucked on the pitch & you were right to beat a man in that devil red shirt with hair & beard black as coal & go back & beat him again just because you could & it was fun & i'd like to tell len shackleton a joke & watch the lines around his eyes crease up as he laughed & i'd like to be there in the crowd of drinkers pulling wee hughie gallacher in a smart suit looking like a boxer or a bookie out of a boozer before kick-off, for these are the stories that i tell my unborn child, my deep voice vibrating underwater in the warm womb as the bairn twists & turns like a neat peter beardsley two-shoe shuffle - i remember imre varadi smashing in a volley at the old gallowgate end, have felt the surge of the crowd down the terrace steps & been squeezed so tight against a barrier that you couldn't get your arms from your side to celebrate, i saw ryan baldacchino, bleached hair, silver boots, score against morton from almost the half-way line, felt the joy of leafing through old match programmes greasy as money with graphic design like old railway posters, have shared a bovril shivering on sidelines with my father, have wandered up dark brick alleys sparkling as water with broken glass with PNE & he's only a poor little hammer & harry roberts is our friend in fading white paint on the walls with my best mate, had the smell of fried onions in my nose, felt the tribal rush running at metal cages chanting, hurled mars bars & shouted judas at a tearful gazza in spurs white shirt, have stood guard outside the dressing room doors in long grey italian coat with folded arms & a frown at a UEFA cup tie as the vultures circled the tunnel & i was there when jimmy glass scored the last-kick-of-the-game winner to keep carlisle in the league, jogging up the pitch in red goalkeeper top & a fella nearby in the paddock grumbling what's he doing? & thinking why not? why not? the bedlam as he lashed the loose ball in. i have seen. i believe.

Sermon

Tripping in the old graveyard
At dawn
The light glinting on the headstones
Resembles the sea
And you preach me a sermon
On the cosmos
The snake eating its tail
Taking care not to step
On the bones of the ancestors
Sunk in the black veiled
Consciousness of purple orange skies
Longing for the sanctuary
Of a hotel bedroom
& the warm familiar grip
Of a wet pussy
To save us from the night.

In B/W

Now watch the moon drown in the sea
As the waves come crashing in
Like some dull, heavy hammer
Dropped on ancient skulls;
The blood runs thick upon the stone.

Whiskey flavoured memories
Of you flicker
Like a surreal film-show
In the ashes of a burnt-out mind.

Some Russian tragedy in black & white.

Broken Spectre

Wild wind battering from all directions & the fear sets in the compulsion to lie flat on wet black Cumbrian slate you can barely see your own boots in the raincloud grey as T.V. static & a terrible howling thousands of feet above sea level clutching desperately at sodden British army camouflage jungle hat to prevent it flying off into the abyss then we're coming down into a spot that is so calm that it is strange & when two men in red cagoules walk past Micky is adamant that they are the Chuckle Brothers & me and Juggers in his fell running gear crack up laughing then we're at a wooden gate that has a sign for the summit & it's like Carry On Up the Khyber & I'm half expecting to see men in red uniforms and kilts lying around massacred with spears in their backs among the bleak tufts of grass it would be no surprise a peculiar circle of rainbow known as a brocken spectre in the moving mist swirling up the precipice of a deep ravine filled with grey scree that's a rare sight in nature & throws our weird long-limbed shadows into the centre we could be in Colorado watching a bear with a coat like burnt honey swiping his broad paw into the frothing white water and snagging the wide silver side of a thick salmon but there ain't no bears in these hills son.

Phase 4

Standing in the neon tunnel, insane,
I seek sanctuary by melting happily
Into her familiar 'Destroy' clothing.
Her body feels more real than ever;
Eyes closed, see the snake,
Smile in the ecstatic recognition of safety
Through the crashing sea
Of a thousand strangers friendly faces.
God, this is so comfortable,
I want to live here.

The collective.

The world of peace and love.
The strangest life we've ever known.

Lazers form a neon grid of squares
In the vast, darkened warehouse.
The heat off the people rises thick
In the distorted music air.
I smile, content, wonder what to say,
And watch the crystals on the wall.

Granny Glasses

She sat in the bar with her long straight black hair in pigtails a Gio-Goi woolly hat black leather gloves & bizarre emerald green tortoise-shell spectacles - with no glass in them her dead granma's she explained they made her feel close to her & they would make a good disguise she was jumping a train to London needed to sort her head out she said & as I swirled the whisky & ice in my glass I recalled the time she told me how when she was a child her mother and father had taken her & her sister for a drive in the country & as she stood at a five-bar gate the others got in the car & drove away with her father telling her that they were leaving her for the gypsies it was a joke & the car stopped within metres but the shock had stayed with her all her life & we had some magical moments lying together in bed hallucinating and giggling on L.S.D. & sharing an amazing almost religious feeling of cosmic consciousness at exactly the same time & for a flash everything in the universe slotted neatly into place & the sudden resounding truth was ours to savour ah, but of course how stupid we've been it's all so simple but as quickly as the answer was revealed it was snatched away & she felt it was like dying & being shown a glimpse of heaven where a white horse was waiting for her & although a Catholic she became increasingly drawn to Buddhism & wouldn't allow anyone to hurt any insects or animals & became quite agitated about it all life seemed so precious to her except her own & when she got on that carriage & it pulled away I was left with that same feeling of loss & bewilderment as when my nana passed away & I wouldn't go & see her laid in state as I thought when you died you became a skeleton picturing the dust rising in a shaft of light through the thick curtains & knocking back the drink that burned in my belly I couldn't help wondering if I was in fact the gypsy they left her for.

Birthday Balloons

The first time I saw this girl I once knew she was blowing up birthday balloons for her sister's surprise party in a fashionable bar all chrome and glass in a former bank building sat on a stool with a tall skinny tattooed Scotsman who was coming down off black microdots & twisted his face in disgust when I ordered a bottle of McEwan's Export hell yeah that brown liquid swirling into the schooner like a swollen river full of spawning salmon & as I kept glancing over at her big blue eyes long lashes face freckled by the African sun & blonde bobbed hair & our gaze finally locked I was struck by the thunderbolt of Sicilian legend so when she asked if we wanted to help I said sure & didn't realise in those first awkward moments that our paths would become intrinsically linked for a while by her sister & months later she'd say that we were soul mates but then her star sign was Cancer & she felt a certain empathy with a bum like me who saw beauty in the light bouncing off those red balloons the empty bottle with foam crawling slowly back down the slender neck the torn beer mats & the lingering lonely fragrance of perfume on an empty pillow.

15 Miles

This old girlfriend's mother took one look & decided that she wasn't going to let me sleep in a bed with her daughter but did offer to lend me a tent to pitch in the back garden so I'm stood at the bottom of the stairs beside a small red shield with crossed swords on the wall & a couple of cats twisting between my ankles purring glancing out of the white net curtains at the flickering orange streetlights throwing long shadows over the tops of shining cars parked outside with an eerie silence like candles in a 1970s power cut with no TV & black bin bags piled high against a grey concrete coal bunker & snow definitely loaded in that black sky but my belly's full of anchovy-topped pizza & I'm wearing a big black lizard skin leather jacket gleaming like vinyl & the girl is warm against me apologising her firm breasts pressed into my chest & the Johnny Walker Black Label fumes are hot on my breath & I think Fuck it I'll walk 15 miles back into the hills & set off leaving behind the last lampposts & big green illuminated road signs seeing the elegant dance of foxes & hearing strange crashing in the woods thinking if you fall asleep in a hedgerow now you'll be found frozen stiff in the salmon pink & pale blue light of morning a monument to stubbornness but then how the hell was I to know about the blackness when the trouble wasn't mine?

Red Fist

Shadows of the red volcano
& the fire of the sun;
The sky is blue
As a blow-torch flame.

We sit cross-legged
On a pebbled beach,
Relics of the early rave scene
Watching rainbows dance
In reflections on a car windscreen;
Wooden beads, white floppy hats,
Minds drowned by old pounding
Acid House & Happy Mondays,
Green bottles glinting grimly
In the sand.

My jeans and work shirt
Are strewn far away
On a threadbare floor.

I am plotting a revolution
Where we crush the bourgeoisie
Like cockroaches on our veranda,
Relishing the dull crack
Of their spineless backs.

What else could I do
But read the Morning Star
& pound red fists on granite walls?

Blood Kit

Old drunk in a beat blue suit with shiny elbows slicked back brylcreemed hair arguing with himself holding a blue five pound note with one hand the other trying to put it back in the silky lining of his inside chest pocket saying have another drink no save it for tomorrow at the end of the bar near the rear door where he always stands a stuffed toy camel beside the till & black leather tick book green neon St. Patrick's Day shamrock glimmering against the optics wobbly glitterball turning shakily on the nicotine yellow ceiling bare wooden floorboards & old church pews a pool table & the flashing lights of a bandit & the joint is full of rough blokes in builders' work clothes flecked in lime & cement dust the locals used to call it the Blood Kit while the old drunk is gesturing wildly to his invisible mate beside him & cursing & no-one pays much attention as his brother goes over head tipped back to peer down his nose through the dirty grey smeared lenses of black framed NHS specs with one leg broken off scruffy wild white beard & hair like a professor gone wrong brown pinstripe jacket fumbling in his pockets & they're mumbling conspiratorially together & big Mick a six foot three farm labourer is pouring pints but he's more at home chucking hay bales like they're light as paper & carrying a sheep under each arm as casually as shopping bags but he's equally happy to carry out any troublemakers in the same fashion & when he gives you a friendly punch on the arm it leaves you wincing in pain a mountain of a man & I swear they'll never invent a machine to replace Mick & two blokes are bar surfing like Hawaii-Five-O while a man with flushed red face dark glasses white moustache & black pork pie hat is nodding his head to the music like the Blues Brothers he's got angina & gives us blasts of Hearty Boom Boom spray under our tongues in the toilets that reek of piss & we're sipping the clear hooch that one of the lads in the Forces has brought back from the Banja Luca Metal Factory Bosnia & although it doesn't actually smell that lethal when you lift up the bottle for closer inspection it leaves a perfect ring on the bar top as it strips the thick old layers of varnish clean down to the naked wood & the vapour makes your eyes water & it doesn't exactly fill you with confidence when you are warned not to spill any on your clothes as you raise the glass cautiously to your lips & you really shouldn't drink anything poured out of an old Barr's glass pop bottle that isn't Irn Bru especially when it's hidden in a brown paper bag under the table & my head is swimming & I nip out of the fire escape to throw up then back in & wash the acidic bile out of my mouth with whisky & as I'm wiping my saliva on the heavy red velvet curtains a dark haired girl who moved away to become a nurse comes over & introduces her boyfriend an Irish actor & singer from North Dublin with a skinhead & goatee beard & menacing eyes who appeared in a Roddy Doyle movie & shakes my hand firmly & says this is my kind of pub.

Circus

I ran off with the show people
& worked on the dodgems; I've surely found my vocation.
It's calm in my caravan at night
under the purple sky & though I still talk in my sleep,
I no longer wake in a sweat.
Burn my suits, I don't need 'em no more.
See you when the moon glints full tilt on the river.

Love
Kid Luck

Night Shift

In a small council bungalow living room with Irish country music playing in the background my uncle's hacking cough as he asks me to make him a cup of tea never asked for anything in his life before hair wet and wild craggy face like Sid James looking very old shirt tails hanging out very unusual for him a proud ex-military man who served in Hong Kong & told me great stories of Port Stanley & char wollahs & Tiger beer & the bastard RSM Connolly a young man in black & white photographs black beret & khaki uniform with his whole life ahead of him & when I say you should get that cough seen to he replies it's the cancer man with an awful certainty that goes off in my head like a hand grenade leaving me numb & all I can come out with is do you want me to get you some space cakes for the pain feeling ridiculous & then the goddamn Post Office make me work a night shift before the funeral tipping wagon loads of grey sacks of mail into containers under the sick yellow light a radio playing tunes to dull the monotony finish at 4am grab a couple of hours sleep then 60 miles journey to the crematorium where the coffin slides through the curtains to Abide with me & back to the red brick Mail Centre for another shift just enough time to get out of black tie & grey Italian coat & into red polo shirt & blue pants snipping the ties and pouring out letters & packets so a couple of nights later I go outside for a cigarette & just keep on walking & wonder who will feed the blackbird that pecks daily at his backdoor for scraps of bread?

Home

In the heat-baked stadium
In Arricife
We sit bored
On large concrete terraces
w/ the sun pinching the skin
On my back
Tighter than a fan belt.

I dream of home;
Dark blue and black clouds
Brewing ominously over Portland Park,
Snow glinting in the floodlights gleam,
Alan Hogg smashing a high drive
Into the loose black and white netting.

The Collier roar…

Border Reiver

The auld alliance is still strong in Paris so as we come out of Pere Lachaise cemetery after gazing at the small grey granite block of Jim Morrison's grave with The Lizard King & Doors lyrics & poems scratched in the sandstone monuments around trying to feel something other than a sense of pilgrimage with large black ravens cawing in the broad leafy cobbled avenues of tombs & before a long trip back on the Metro I cross the road into a sinister dark garage that smells of oil & diesel with spanners & tools lying around and a Citroen bonnet open looking to change a large Franc note & the burly unshaven middle-aged mechanic in dirty blue overalls smoking a strong cigarette eyes me suspiciously in long grey Crombie coat & Levi jeans & asks Americain? Anglais? with disdain & a hint of disgust in his voice but I'm no mug & thinking on my feet reply Non monsieur Je suis Ecossais so his attitude instantly changes & his eyes light up & a broad grin crosses his face & he slaps my shoulder as he growls in appreciation & slowly & deliberately counts out every centime to prove he's not ripping me off & I'm suddenly struck with the revelation that my sheep stealing ancestors used this very trick on the borders centuries ago with no allegiance to either the St. George or St. Andrew's cross just whatever is going to get you by & kind of satisfied that I've conned the mechanic & I'm thinking that Morrison had a Scottish heritage too & he'd have enjoyed the moment & it isn't until we get home & look at our black & white photographs of the graveside that we notice a strange white shadow like a shed adder skin up the tomb alongside that looks exactly like Morrison's profile.

One More Tab

A white pony appeared
At the dark window
like an apparition.

I can't take much more
Of these late night sessions
In Bob's 'Viper Rooms'.

One more tab then bed

White surf crashes in
On industrial shores.
Scarred by Belfast
She stares into the sea

Reclaiming Goa.

Journey into Space

We're on a job at a plush country hotel long red gravel drives hewn from the scar in the green hills at Biddlestone all trees & private golf course taking the glass out of a old conservatory before we take it down me in jeans & worn steel toe-capped boots fur-lined cord jacket to keep out the cold chill Charlie with his beard & blue cigarette smoke & red & black checked coat chipping expertly at the putty with a hammer & chisel wooden ruler jutting out of his back pocket I'm a little dazed after just a couple of hours sleep reaching up and holding the large panes in tough leather work gloves as he passes them down but after we've sat down for our bait out of old army canvass bags stewed lukewarm tea in flasks the bread soggy on cheese sandwiches in an empty loaf bag wrapping in the beat-up old green van that smells of cement dust & wood shavings seats with their foam guts hanging out the heating cranked up I start feeling really groggy & the high-pitched constant tone in my head starts to get worse sweat running down my forehead limbs weak and shaky & I have to go to some bushes to throw up expecting to feel better but then the tone turns to a constant chatter of voices in my head ringing and spinning and I have to tell Charlie I've got to go for a walk & curl up under a tree thinking how I'm going to ask him to take me to the mental hospital 10 miles down the road as I just can't stop these voices jabbering rubbish feeling very unreal and scared as it doesn't pass & swearing to myself I'll never drink Newcastle Brown Ale again & this is the worst hangover ever.

Pigeon

On a building site where I was grafting we found a pigeon nesting on a shot-blasted wall sitting on the gleaming white eggs one hatched & when the ceiling fixers two big fat Scousers started putting in boards we shifted the yellow squeaker chick onto a cutting of plasterboard on a window ledge outside & the chick grew & flourished surrounded by the roar of diggers & generators & a site of 40 burly men & it reminded me of dark winter nights when my Dad would return from work with an old army bag containing his bait box & putty knifes slung over his shoulder & we'd go down & start scraping the wooden floorboards of the loft with rusty coal shovels in the eerie half-light of a paraffin burner the soft cooing of the birds as we first entered with a loud click of the latch then the fleeting applause of a bird's wings as it flapped down from it's nesting box as the soft light burst into the darkness with a whoosh & the rattle that the beans made as I scooped them from an old Ceylon Tea chest in a SMA baby milk tin then the tiny roar like a thousand marbles as I poured them into the feeders with the soft feathers of the birds brushing against my hand as they jostled for a prime spot the smell of gloss paint on the auld fella's multi-colour splattered white overalls & a crisp crinkle & aromatic waft of Virginian tobacco as he lit a tab with the dog end glowing orange in the gloom but just as the squeaker was losing the last of it's down I went to check one morning & the bird was frozen stiff as concrete how tight is that to die one day before you could fly?

Two Steps Back

Hard to believe that 16 years after I quit the post office I'd be back in pale blue shirt & dark work pants humping a heavy sack up & down red brick terraces leaving a trail of snapped elastic bands & cursing under my breath at packages that won't squeeze through letterboxes & feeling the rage build as I pull out another bundle of junk mail that people don't want to receive & I certainly don't want to carry & standing grim-faced at a grey plastic fitting in the sorting office with mounting trays of letters that just don't seem to go down no matter how hard I concentrate on winging them into the numbered slots while talking football betting horse racing boxing & women with the rest of the boys & hoping that maybe I'll catch even just a glimpse of a housewife's tits while out on the walk to keep myself motivated but I'm still last out of the office despite not swaying so bad with the drink & gear it was like working the mail trains or having The Eagles pumped out at low volume for easy listening like the last time & it still feels like I've taken two huge steps back even if I can imagine the black tarmac blurring by my feet is gems shining on black water on nights of no moon with the mermaid queen just under the surface her name is Nyai Loro Kidul & her number is 327 or see the Sphinx in my mind instead of the pale sandstone of a house as I plod heavy-booted up the drive but these thoughts don't seem to flash through the collective consciousness of the postal service who'll work them dreams outta ya boy but then I can come over all calm & pass a bush full of excitable chattering chaffinches on a fresh spring morning & everything feels like it will look after itself.

For Real

The American tourists,
All cameras and ski jackets,
Looked on incredulous
As my 3-year-old boy
Spat on the Heart of Midlothian.
'Is this for real?' one drawled.
George Tait of the Stankford
Locked up in the stinking tollbooth
Because his sons
In steel helmets and leather jacks
Left a man who was ploughing on their land
For dead.
Aye, we're for real.

Pedal Power

I remember vividly my first bike a canary yellow Boxer brand new Christmas morning 1978 smelling of fresh rubber tyres & oiled metal & the pride I felt as my mother took photographs while I coasted down the estate with one hand free trying to look cool in brown cords & cream shirt with huge collars & greasy para's crap hat that I even slept in & the madness of our bike rides as kids like the wacky races on an assortment of second-hand Grifters & Choppers & some on a sister's bike too small & with a basket on the handlebars or a racer too big & uncontrollable wobbling down the road while we turned up the mudguards onto the wheels so it made a noise like a motorbike as we pedalled & one of the lads putting his ear to the tarmac like an American Indian to listen for traffic before we flew around a blind corner & the time I could hear clanking as I sped down a steep hill & looked down to see a metal clothes hanger stuck in my spokes before it jammed against my brake blocks & catapulted me into the air over the rider in front & bouncing down the road on my face & the great event when Dangerous Brian made 8 of us younger boys lie on the street as he attempted to break an Eval Kineval record by leaping us off a wooden ramp & as he pedalled furiously towards us I could almost imagine him in the red white & blue of a Captain America style suit & helmet & the rear wheel crashing down on the smallest lad at the end who went home very quietly & didn't tell his mother for two days that he was in pain & had in fact broken his collarbone but then they used to build us tough in Northumberland & we wore the bruises with pride as another step in the making of man.

Playing with Snakes

Sneaking past a secluded loggers hut with two older blood brothers the sweet smell of fresh sawn wood & wet forest mould in our nostrils & knots in our stomachs like when your father threw you in the air as a kid & waited until the very last second to catch you or stealing just a glimpse of a Stobhill lass that you're hot for in class with your heart skipping a beat & pounding in your chest & the ripsaw tears through the timber with a scream & you've got mud flecked on your black school pants skiving for the day again just striding right on past the queues at the bus stop & away up onto the hill the excitement of freedom tinged with the fear of getting caught & we find an upturned boat in the overgrown green foliage among the bulrushes & get the nerve up to sail it across to an island with grey low morning mist still on the icy water & improvised paddles slopping & when we reach the small tree-covered land spray a bush silver with a can of car paint & I'm struck by that same sense of trepidation that I would feel a few years later when we first tried LSD & the vivid memory of the Coquetdale poet John French Jackson is firmly in my mind a painter & decorator by trade in his white bib & brace & a dark suit jacket with his face tanned & ruddy from the Northumbrian weather lined like a currant & his shock of white hair in sharp contrast a spark in his eyes as he laughed & how he was also a former champion Army boxer who played the mouth organ & dipped it in his pint & stopped me at the top of some steps known as Jacob's Ladder & asked Wheor ye gannin', son? & when I answered Aa'm away to scheul, Jackie he replied Whey, ye divn't waant to dee that, man. Gerraway up on yon hill an' playuh wi the snayiks & how the wisdom evaded me at the time & yet it could just about be the greatest lesson ever taught.

Family Tree

My grandma said I was nowt but a rogue
when I was just a bit bairn
and I thought that was a bad thing
until I did the family tree
and found the long line of rogues
that I was descended from through her
like Adam Scott 'The King of Thieves'
hung from a tree outside his own door,
like Robert Scott that took his axe to the oak
of a church and murdered a fella
he was at feud with inside,
like the Scotts that happed up someone's land
and smashed their plough up as a warning.
A succession of heavy drinking hill farmers
with ten kids from the upland wastes

Only then did I realise
that she was claiming me
as one of her own.

Only then did I know
that she was laughing inside
when she caught me telling my cousin
I wasn't afraid of a fucking bull.

March or Die

Sturdy canvass hiking boots lift with a wet suck as they pull up out of the boggy trail that smells of peat & rotting wet bracken & wonderful dark earthy mud & you're scanning instinctively for a route up to the summit as you pass a roaring waterfall of melting snow through the bleak leafless skeletons of twisted grey trees thankful for the lined ski jacket & black wool cap with your face tingling from exertion & you're thinking It's not meant to be easy & pulling at the rough tops to drag yourself up the steep ravine as you receive sudden bursts of energy before lying enveloped in a soft bed of purple heather for a breather & throwing a handful of nuts & raisins down your throat that instantly reinvigorate your aching muscles & the isolation is wonderful & you're really testing yourself against nature grabbing handholds on grey lichen-covered limestone outcrops with thighs burning then you're at a little stone cairn with amazing views of the rounded desolate Scottish highland mountains just taking it all in with a sense of satisfaction & achievement as snow brews in the pale grey sky & a wind whips in so strong that you crouch low against the ground avoiding the edge of the precipice then finding a break & bouncing down off the top & washing your face in a fresh mountain burn that's so cold your hands & face burn & a startled grouse flusters into the air with a distress call then you start shuffling down a vertical slope through the denser woods on loose rock when you hear the barking of a deer & are amazed as a majestic red doe wanders cautiously nose sniffing the air by below you flattened on cold stone holding your breath tightly & you are just so pleased that you left behind the wooden chalets & steam rooms & wine bottles & luxury of modern living to get out into the wilderness & how you couldn't just sit on your ass while wearing a tan French Foreign Legion T-shirt of the 2EME R.E.P with skull & crossbones & the legend Le Diable Marche avec vous.

Dirty Jobs

Heavy metal drain cover drops with a dull clang as the bald-headed plumber in checked flannel work shirt baseball cap LA Lakers T-shirt & gold chain looking like a WWF wrestler stands twisting lengths of plastic rods together & we eye the thin trickle of water down the glazed orange tubes while discussing his cheap beach holidays in Bulgaria & visits to Miami trying not to think too much about the job ahead first thing Monday morning & still a bit hung-over with cigarette packet on the van dashboard alongside copper fittings & a pack of talcum-powder lined rubber gloves that we snap on automatically & I have an irrational fear lurking in the back of mind that a black rat is going to spring out of the darkness of the subterranean pipes & tear at my face spreading disease & bubonic plague & black death & the rods begin sliding up easily to begin with as the plumber twists & prods them & I screw new lengths on as they disappear when they suddenly stop & with a couple of hefty rams a dreadful gurgle & bubbling erupts & the plumber is frantically pulling back the rods when we're overwhelmed by a disgusting yellow brown slurry like a stinking porridge racing up & over the man hole & flooding down the tarmac bits of white & pink tissue paper & used tampons clinging to the surface & our rubber boots with a gag reflex forcing your stomach into your mouth & the awful stench of human waste overripe in the air & we're literally wading through shit to put a roll of greasy notes in our pockets & bread on the table.

Haunted

I am haunted by ghosts of pastel backstreets lit at night.
They're there in my head.
I'm lazy.
Maybe this one time I should just get in the car
and drive up into the Highlands
and got lost amongst the mist and mountains.

Simple pleasures –
the sound of a bottle of whisky getting uncapped,
the first bright flick of a cigarette lighter.
Still these ghosts wake me in a sweat.

The dark outline of a nipple through a white t-shirt.
Can't you see my lizard hide, these reptilian eyes?
Her swollen clitoris invited my tongue to play.
Strange shapes in the darkness.
My carcass bloated and swollen in a leather jacket.
The scent of fresh citrus fruits and wine.
Leave a warm impression in the bed
when you depart.

Boom of the Bass

The dying summer sun receding on the confused faces of grey suited commuters scurrying past the lofty Victorian elegance of Newcastle Central Station grey streets grey buildings charred & blackened by some long lost Industrial age grey pigeons flapping in the rafters then a mad splash of pastel colours lilac hooded tops & the faded denim of 24" flares with white frayed bottoms from trailing on the tarmac & white cricket hats & whistles & ice pops & happy faces & laughter a throng of idle chatter & a buzz of excitement as the buses begin filling & pulling away through high narrow streets over the green iron web of the Tyne Bridge up the sloping streets of Gateshead & on towards the setting sun with fast fading rays flashing on the windscreen on towards the smoking chemical stacks of Teesside & eventually pulling up at a large warehouse with a heaving dancing crowd outside & large handmade flowered banners proclaiming 1989 The Second Summer of Love hands reaching for the sky & a tinny rhythm of blasting whistles drifting on the air & striding with mounting excitement through large doors & into the blackness with a piercing solitary neon green laser spinning in the dark & an ice cream van enveloped in the dense fog of a smoke machine & the heavy steady throb of the boom of the bass.

Regrets

Still gutted that I never got to play on Portland Park & yet on all those hung-over Sunday mornings anticipating the dreaded knock on the door that meant shoving clarty boots into a plastic Co-op bag with the stench of damp shin-pads grass & sizzling bacon unable to face a fry-up as soon as I squeezed into the car already full of four farting team-mates the gaffer would promise we were playing on the pitch only to roll up at Peoples' Park or Flower Park & the only time I did get on the hallowed turf was when some big dirty bastard from Alnwick jumped through me two-footed & I was sent to the General Hospital for X-Rays on a suspected broken ankle & wor lass dragged us to the Tuesday market for new kex & all that tight drying mud and dog shite on your knees & picked out of the hairs on your shins in the pub afterwards was in vain when the council sold the ground to make way for another fucking supermarket unsettling the ghosts of the sepia teams.

Cosmic Gratitude

Mist snaking slow & low down the river valley at dawn with steams of pink sky just peering over the ominous black shapeless hills that loom in the darkness & dew still wet on the grey grass just finished a shift at the bakery with the heady smell of warm bread still in my nostrils & the clanking noise of a wrapping machine & blaring radio in my head in those slightly unreal hours where everything is just like a dream under buzzing strip lights walking back to the house with the colour drained from everything like a old fading black & white photograph wearing a little white cap with a cheese stick loaf wrapped in grease proof paper under my arm ready to curl up against the hot skin of a naked curvy brunette in a comfortable bed when I come across a fox on the road hit by a car his fine red coat suddenly very real against the negative light his eyes closed & breathing laboured & heavy & rasping blood congealed on his snout & curled lip showing teeth the course hairs on his back rising erratically & shallow obviously beyond help & I'm struck by the quandary of thinking should I snap his neck to put him out of his pain but there's no way I can kill an animal with my bare hands so I quietly talk him down & stroke his head & though I know foxes are naturally wary of humans I'm overcome with sadness & compassion so I move the warm shaking body gently off the tarmac & onto the grass by a hedgerow hoping that it feels more natural & I sit on the road talking quietly until his breathing stops & with a heavy heart I'm hoping that I've given the fox some comfort in it's final moments & though I'm not a religious man I'm wondering if in some Shamanic way the foxes spirit has been released & a few days later as we drive around the bend on the road & I'm retelling the story to the brunette girl behind the wheel I just catch a glimpse of the white tip of a red tail darting into the thick green gorse bushes on the hillside opposite & am very suddenly reminded that life goes on & although I don't mention it I take comfort in the belief it was some form of cosmic gratitude from the fox & a weight suddenly lifts from my shoulders.

Haircut

The shop next door is boarded up
there's brylcreem and black plastic combs
by the old wooden counter
& knackered leather seats in front of the mirror.

We plonk you down
squirming, unsure,
a black cloak wrapped around you,
your blonde hair clipped off
in little swishes from the scissors.

There's a lad with a black eye
getting his head shaved
in the seat next door
& he reckons there'll be murders
as he got his ribs kicked in by a gang.

So when he gives you the thumbs up
as you turn to watch & giggle,
I know you'll be sound as a salmon
fighting your way back up the Coquet
white water to spawn.

Picket Line

Shoulders hunched against the gritty wind in a high collared black maritime coat with the glint of a small silver and red enamel union pin double snake & birds wings on breast flap standing with hands deep in jeans pockets leaning against cold metal railings of the works' entrance mind focused on the brightly coloured old miners' lodge banners of my childhood ornate as working men's club membership cards in brown leather holders or Up North Combine pigeon race certificates & colliery brass bands & men in donkey jackets with orange NCB flashes & white helmets & the battles they had with lines of policemen with clear plastic riot shields & batons thinking how did I ever get so bothered about graft when I really just want to stare into the blackness at a smoky spinning neon green lazer tunnel feeling my heart pounding in my throat with the industrial grind of hardcore techno throbbing in my ears sweat dripping off the ceiling & the cold touch of blue & brown plastic love beads on my chest but then my grandad's words of wisdom that you never cross a picket line ring in my ears & I shout scab with the rest of them with great gusto.

Hillside

Old beams white and cracked
as empty whisky barrels
and long gone
are my ribcage.

Crumbling sandstone blocks
blackened by rain
then eroded by sad, howling winds
off the Cheviot tops
tumbled down
high as clouds, exposed on dewy green
as the years erase the names.

Andrew alias Dand
Dand the Baillie
Dand the Burgess
Borgwell

Blood locked in the landscape
sheep bleating, faces black as Presbyterian ministers,
a gang of long-legged lambs lolloping,
scattering chaffinches from a hedgerow,

This scar on the hillside is a scar on my face.
These coping stones cowped on edge my bones.

The Egg Shack

I'm gonna give all this up & move somewhere hot & open up a place down on the beach called The Egg Shack all bare grey weather-washed boards like driftwood real laid-back with a sign in a swirling font similar to Coca-Cola & a red pan tile roof with a big old juke box in the corner & a couple of cold beers on tap & the sands will be so white & soft it'll be like walking through sugar with a hammock around the back slung up between two palms & a few chickens in a hutch & I'll be at the hot plate in blue & white checked chefs pants & a surfing T-shirt & red bandana rustling up omelettes & boilers & scramblers & French toast with the Happy Mondays playing low out of the speakers & a green beer bottle in one hand & we'll laugh when American sailors in white uniforms come in & sing She's lost that loving feeling to girls in bikinis at the bar like in Top Gun & while watching the soccer on Sky Sports I'll remember shivering in biting cold press boxes with a phone hot on my ear ringing through frantic copy loaded with hyperbole to the sports desk & the time a grey-haired old England International wrapped up in a scarf & flat cap turned to me at a ramshackle Scottish Third Division ground with beat plastic seats & rusting steel & corrugated sheets & said shaking his head & chuckling I once played at the Olympic Stadium in Rome as he poured some rum & coffee known as gunfire from a flask & we'll kick a ball around in the white breakers gently rolling up on the shore with conches for goalposts the sun setting orange & purple on the horizon & make string necklaces from shells that we'll give away to costumers who'll forget the mighty dollar work pressures economic decline global warming the crisis of capitalism & come back year on year.

Bitter End

If I came home from work
With a canvas bait bag slung over the shoulder,
And my house had been hit by a missile
Red brick rubble strewn on the street
Broken glass and slates and cement dust
A hole blown in the terrace
Allowing blue skies and clouds
To peer through
My family inside
You can rest assured that
I'd pick up a Kalashnikov or RPG
And hit back.
Keep fighting to the bitter fucking end.
In Gaza, in Kabul, in Carlisle.

That's not terrorism.
That's Love.

Comparing Tattoos

There's rough laughter & dirty jokes as I'm comparing tattoos with the lads up the beat old wooden staircase of the plumbers' workshop all spilt brass fittings & coils of grey plastic pipe & old engines & wooden boxes filled with copper off-cuts to cash in for the Xmas party bonus off the scrap man with yellowing page 3 pin-ups on the walls & grease & oil under our fingernails & my traditional gypsy's head & swallow are beaten by an impressive full sleeve of American Indian designs hidden under the blue boilersuit of an electrician while the boss is on the phone behind a desk with clutter all around him & blue grey smoke from cigarettes stubbed in an overflowing ash tray so he tells us a job's come in & to get on it while writing down an address then asks me to stick a tenner on a 25-1 shot at the bookies over the road & peels a note off a greasy roll from his pocket & it's just another day in the building trade with a war on 4,000 miles away where some guys are laughing raucously & comparing tattoos in a large green tent with oiled machine guns on a table & shiny brass cartridge cases lying around & one blokes' traditional skull & dagger is beaten by an impressive full sleeve Chinese dragon design hidden under the desert camouflage of a gunners' fatigues while the sergeant is on the field telephone & tells the boys a job's come in so they pull on their helmets & start checking clips & going out to take a gamble in a thin metal bottomed APC that can't take the impact of a rocket attack & they're not keen on chancing a flutter not at them odds kidda.

Dawn

cackle of crows
marks the dawn
fox
laboured breathing from
crushed body
still warm and wet w/ dew
shaking fearful animal
its blood mingled with mine
heavilly intoxicating
& high as heaven
i became a fox
i look out thru alert black eyes
the world is very strange
& full of prey
i'm sniffing in the bushes
my wet snout in the air.

The Girl from the Scree Hills
& the Girl from the Red City

I

'She dances headlong in the stars,
chasing dreams in stolen cars...'
back on tyneside
three wheels spin in a circle of fire
the streets are ridged like a lizards back
gleaming cars roar thru yellow smoke
green bridge stretched over black water
features pulled hard as a coal face
three times he went under
& came up coughing flowers.
foul words a scratched in the dust & blood
of the concrete veins of a city.
touching the warm body w/ electric
fingertips
thru the exhaustion of many days
travel in the sluggish heat
we race toward a climax.
two magpies dodge invisible objects
on top of a black chimney stack.
sinking into the soft upholstery
of a super Nova
w/ a girl from the red city
& a girl from the scree hills
when they smile
it's like the first golden sunlight
across the wet grass of dawn.
Got to get back
to the purple hills of the border.
I lay down this wild curse
on the grey suited men in BMWs
that have invaded our homelands.
"the orange flames shall roar

thru the tortured frames of yr soft flesh
the crows shall peck yr eyes from their sockets
i have returned w/ sunburned skin
to stamp on yr throats w/
boots encaked in building site mud.
to wrap yr heads in barbed wire,
to infect yr PCs w/ weird viruses."
i demand a mexican rug.
you can keep yr space age hoovers
yr pension schemes, yr shitty jobs,
yr platinum credit cards.
i just want to fly.
Full of vodka
took ten tokes off a coke-can bong
& fell spinning back
into the void.

II

dim headlights flashed across a wall
& the girl from the red citys smile
illuminated the dark & stormy sea
in one huge swinging arc.
a chemical plant in Cumbria
in the weird cigarette-smoke blue light
seen from high speeds
of a flashing carriage.
the girl from the scree hills
dissects the space
around my consciousness
like a sleek black panther
stalking the night...
cranes
boarded up shop fronts
left the mogadon
on botchergate.
the girl from the red city
thru a careless sideways hex
as he strode aimlessly
thru the dawn city streets
to the fleeting applause
of a startled pigeons wings.

got to get back
to the purple hills of the border.
the girl from the scree hills awoke
to the sound of sparrows
pecking putty from the windowpane.
wide-eyed as a shaman
stumbled thru wet moss
clawed at calloused bark,
how can i see thru these dancing trees
with white fog in my eyes ?
the girl from the scree hills
& the girl from the red city

nurse my broken spirit
w/ chardonay, w/ jack daniels whiskey,
bottles of rolling rock, horse linament,
olive oil, wd-40, rosehip,
microchips & clockfaces,
test-tubes & chemicals,
drowned by the moonlight
& the certainty of chance.
the damp earth
soaked into the fabric of my jeans
as i fell to my knees,
a decorated veteran of the psychedelic wars.

I Can Tell You the Names

I can tell you the names of the heroes of old pit villages,
pub brawlers and poachers,
the streets all named after revolutionaries –
Marx Avenue, Lenin Place –
their stern faces on long disused union banners,
red in dusty halls,
hauled out once a year to lead
the old colliery brass band down hills.
There are flat-capped men here
who can recall the red flag
flying from the town hall,
bold against the blue sky filled with pigeons
circling for home and the loft,
tough men, forged from the hardships
of the General Strike and hunger marches
and they'll give you the hammer and sickle, bonny lad,
the hammer smashing your knuckles and the sickle in your guts.
The Soviet Union gave the pitmen here
something to believe in,
black from the coal face,
cobbled streets gleaming wet with rain,
and if the National Health Service is their legacy
then hell, they did OK.

Dark Country Night

Street light through a crack in the curtains
the squeaking floorboards on the risers
& yourself, roused from deep dreams,
with hair stood on end, rubbing bleary eyes,
as your father, back from the pub,
carries you downstairs in a fireman's lift,
& unfurls a hedgehog from his builders' palm
that hurries across the floor nose in the air
then curls into a ball tight as a hairbrush
while the old fella pulls a cold bottle of Coke
from the pocket of his warm site coat.

We hail these simple magic moments
of the dark country night
with a small smile, a knowing wink.

No words.

Lost

the saddest sight Harry's seen
since he came off the speed
is a racing pigeon pecking
among the fag-ends on the pavement
outside McDonald's
pining for the ducket,
his partner sitting on plastic eggs
anxious for his return.

We Are Hill People

Make a voodoo doll of me from straw
and stuff it with dead, red bracken
purple heather and old beech leaves.

We are forged
not from the wind that howls and moans
down river valleys gurgling brown
as ale with deep salmon pools
and leaps made famous by old reivers
laden down with a sheep on their back
that cowped them in and felt that gurling,
cold water choking in the lungs,
but from whisky stills
tinged with peat
and smoke ripe as Craster kippers,
that golden spirit burning in our bellies.

We are hill people.

Dangerous as the Afghan-Pakistan border
though instead of tribesmen
in red dog-tooth scarves and camouflage jackets
with Kalashnikov rifles and blocks of marijuana
in cellophone wrapping
we had steel bonnets and pikes and swords
and a lust for revenge and murder
that gave the words blackmail, bereave and scot-free
to the English language.

The border reivers were the original mafia
think Goodfellas with leather jerkins instead of Armani suits
rough Border accents instead of Italian
lamb stew instead of meatballs and tomato sauce
Robert De Niro as Johnnie Armstrong
Joe Pesci as Adam 'The Pecket' Scott
striking fear into the Anglo-Scottish wilds
running in crews of 400 strong.

When a Border child is christened,
his right hand is excluded from the ceremony
so he can deal out blows for the Family
without fear of Holy retribution.

We are hill people.

We've seen dawns lit up
with the orange flames of farm houses
had the charred flesh in our noses
and felt the tight grip of the noose
around our necks
and the choking cold water
filling our lungs.

We are hill people.

Red

I had visions
of a Red Star on top
of the Houses of Parliament.

Bronze statues of Arthur Scargill
and Mick McGahey in the bustling squares
of London.

Hallucinations of parades down Edinburgh's Royal Mile.
Rockets, tanks and soldiers marching in green uniforms
giving clenched fist salutes
to the men in the sensible suits and fur-lined Cossack hats
waving from the balcony
as 'The Internationale' plays from the speakers,
the needle scratchy on the pick-up.

Britain loves a good ceremony.

I see a green statue of Karl Marx
on the end of the Tyne Bridge,
Leon Trotsky replacing Earl Grey
with the 'Socialist Worker' paper sellers
busying themselves at the foot of the stone plinth.

Reading the Morning Star
in a busy state-owned coffee shop
with the bust of Lenin in the windows
and Antonio Gramsci's face on crumpled red fivers.

The hammer and sickle on old metal post boxes,
telephone kiosks and postmen's uniforms.
The red flag flapping in the breeze
on hotel entrances, public buildings, libraries.

I can picture the Gulags in the Welsh mountains
where they hold show trials
for our Class enemies.

Maggie Thatcher.
Bankers.
Insurance firm owners.
Energy Company directors.
The Tory party
Swinging from the end of a rope.

The Royals can stay
But must pay their own way.
Elizabeth as a school dinner lady in tabard
puffing on a tab round the back by the bins;
Philip grafting under cars on his back
as a mechanic in blue grease-smeared
boiler suit.

All I wanted to do
was work for the union.

Never mind the careers advisor
sat in the office that smelt of cigarettes and coffee
with sour breath, his hair in a long mullet
and large aviator rimmed glasses.

Fuck you, I thought.

Have you considered the Army?
There's a whole host of opportunities
for young men like yourself
in the Armed Forces.

Aye, plenty of opportunities
to get yourself blown up.

Grain

This auld fella's grain runs as tight
as the mahogany unloaded from
grimy ships at tyne dock.
he was raised in bustling noise
where blokes in cloth caps smoking woodines
with bits of bodies blown off in the trenches
& buckshee wooden legs & hands stand around
like a lowry painting
as the cranes swang in goods from hot distant lands.

union banners & social clubs
the blackness of the pit
dark as jet
mourning broaches of victorian ladies
or guinness.

the iron lady? maggie fucking thatcher?
don't make me laugh

these men were born in adversity
& thought the russian revolution
would liberate them from outdoor netties
& tin baths in the front room
the squalor
six kids top to toe in the bed
& the dreaded T.B.

they're harder than three coffin nails
brayed home with a riveter's hammer, man.

Sick

I haven't seen this much puke
since the time I drank 1.5 litres
of rot-gut red wine in 30 minutes
and lay incapable on a beer garden bench
with the whole world shaking
or when I recall flashes
on my hands and knees
belly full of brandy
wailing at the moon
the stars
hot chunks splattering the pavement
or hugging the cool white porcelain
in a sweat each heave relieving the spins
or waking sprawled on the grass
a notebook smeared in mud
ill with the whisky
and the only words I could read
from the unintelligible scrawl was
'so many birds at dawn'
that pale grey light
moist with the dew
and when you come back to reality
its all bankers
and politicians
and shit jobs
and enough to make a man sick.

Just like Oz

When I was a bairn
I wanted to be just like Oz
In *Auf Wiedersehen, Pet*
Slugging stubbies of cold Heineken
In a bomber jacket, combat pants and boots
While slapping down the top course of bricks
And not giving a flying fuck about the ganger.

I wanted to play darts in a site hut
That stunk of fried eggs and stale socks
Sink pints in rough bars chasing frauleins
And enjoy the camaraderie of the building game
Among the dust and chugging generators
Calling the German lads *'Erik's'* and cracking jokes
About the War.

I wanted to be a bloke
A Gateshead hard case
Wolf-whistling at the firm bounce of a secretary's breasts
As she walked past the scaffolding with a spirited step

I'm peering down your top right now.

Thunderflash

Here they come
the Gremlins
bouncing across the street
in jeans, stone island jackets, Burberry scarves & baseball caps
arms outstretched & gesturing
shouting: 'haway then, let's have it!'
as older blokes in leather coats with shaved heads
stream out from the bar decked in union jack flags
& start hurling pint glasses that smash on the tarmac

the buzz is building
a low tension like electricity in rain
it's exciting

as a thunderflash goes off with a bang
blue smoke streams out of a canister in the road
& a cheer goes up

United! United!

Railroad

Bob Crow in his brown baker boy leather flat cap has turned the collars on his wool coat up as he stands on the picket lines outside a London underground station & if there's any hope for this country then it's men like Bob the railwaymen's secretary that will bring about the change but then the railwaymen have always been progressive with their 'workers of all countries unite' pin badges & although the miners had the reputation for militancy it's the lads that worked the tracks and engines that were always leading figures in the labour movement & it's getting diluted the less industrial workers that are left with the party full of white collar workers and computer geeks & suburban suits whose biggest struggle has been getting a cappuccino machine in the bait room no longer the grind of steel on steel the smoke chuffing along countryside hedgerows with wind whistling freely through the hair grease and oil on a blue boilersuit & I come from a railway family with my great grandfather working his way up from the stock sheds to a signalman & beat hero Neal Cassady worked the coaches with his punch clipping tickets from San Francisco down the Californian coast or leapt off with his blocks of wood to splinter under the wheels as a brakeman in torn leather gloves & a red bandana to wipe the sweat from his brow & it's all real graft that leaves a man satisfied & ready for ham and eggs and a slurp of coffee out of a tin mug & it's the industrial workers that will fight the class war not call centre staff & students & college lecturers man.

Warning

beware the british hitler
he's out there
somewhere
hidden behind the curtains of a suburban street
behind the union jack
maybe he has a stupid moustache
& hair brylcreemed flat
& his mam has ironed creases in his jeans
but he's out there
somewhere
hating the yids the pikeys the pakis
the wogs the commies
he hates you
with a heart
as black as stout.

Starlings

Sitting on the end of a single bed
in the dark wearing headphones
listening to *The Who*
in a green German army parka
with a union jack sewn on the back
wanting to be as reckless as Jimmy
imagining the sea rolling on pebbles at Brighton
& wishing that you had a GS scooter
& a girl with black bobbed hair brown eyes
an American fishtail coat & hold-ups
wanting to belong to something
wishing that you could use schizophrenia or the pills
as an excuse for standing dark eyed in the kitchen
alone, staring, the party reeling around you in a blur
not realising that you're all as free as starlings
chattering in the trees, fleeing in a fluttering whoosh
into skies tinged with the smell of coal smoke.

Fate

We are the people below deck,
the doomed spectres of a ghostly crew
that flip cards from Tarot decks
& perform Ouija boards,
summoning devils in ritual black magic,
desperate for visions.

Pentangles scratched in chalk
on the wooden boards
that can call up the fierce eyes of a figurehead
flashing real as lightening
or the sudden illumination of a slot machine
at the strange, broken memories
of a boom like thunder
rumbling around her once smooth flesh,
now stolen in oak.

A red-haired girl
that reminds you of some slattern in a Victorian bar,
breasts heaving in a tight-laced top
a wicked twinkle in her eyes, green as a cats,
a woman in the window wet with rain,
the warmth of liquor in my belly
and the hot touch of her skin,
pussy slippery as Port,
the moon still hanging full and bright in the wild air.

Cargo hold stuffy as a museum
rammed with relics and icons –
a mummified Egyptian prince
with his face set in a perpetual scream,
Inca gold face masks glimmering in the darkness,
Masonic treasure marked with the pyramid and all-seeing eye,
grim, grinning, Mexican death dolls,
Judas' lost Gospel,
souls cast adrift with our terrible cache ….
and we can't unload it.

Waved on, we sail pass the lonely lighthouses
and feel the low, sad moan of the foghorn
penetrate our very souls
as no port will allow us to dock up,
some strange hallucinatory vibrations
darkening our passage
merely from the fact the bottle didn't break when she was named.

So we cast off back into the sea
bobbing on the breakers like an old rum bottle.

This is our wretched fate.

Hot Trod

D'ynaa Youngy, back then
wu'd huv driven ten beast lowin,
billowing snorted breath & white rollin eyes,
through a pass in the Cheviots
wi rain lashing vortical,
ya daft grin hidden
under the shadus of a Spanish steel bonnet
waater drippin off the rim
& a mist thickaa than a settling pint
On horseback in leather jacks
wi flintlocks and swords,
the green grass flattened & weirdly bright at dawn
the scent of bornt thatched roofs in wor hair
& women on wor calloused hands
Evor riding, evor riding,
The hunting horns o' the March Warden's men
echoing up the valley.

No heavy weight of history
as wuh played wi star spangled Evel Knievel toys
& plastic soldiers in a fort, laughin,
in tight *Star Wars* T-shirts & cord flares,
& ya grey smudged presence is still theor
In the blustering rain
in this wind whistling through the rough grass tops
& shaking the bows of fir trees;
pickin horses at the bookies,
keepin steady watch ower the bairns.

Full Moon

It must be a full moon judging by the state of some of the lunatics that are out tonight their bony faces illuminated alternately lime green and hell red by the lights & as you watch them grinding their jaws you realise that half of them are descended from such notorious characters *as archie fire the braes* & *fingerless will* & *nebless clem* & *buggerback* it's no surprise that they are off their nuts & dealing gear in the darkness when *geordie burn* admitted he'd spent his whole time whoreing drinking & taking deep revenge for slight offences & on some of those nights sitting beside a girl with glitter eye shadow & black lycra running shorts in a hot dark nightclub with sweat running down the walls & dripping off the ceiling that felt like they would never end as you were absolutely caught in the moment which was frozen in time & the incredible rushes off the speed as the hardcore biorhythms threatened to spin the top of your head clean off & the metallic futuristic music bleeping & droning although even as you stroke her hot goose-bumped skin & talk of peace & love & empathy there is an explosive temper just below the surface that could blow at any minute & you have to think that the although the clock moves on some things never change.

Best Get Drunk

There is no God
No supreme being
to absolve your sins.
Just an energy
in the rocks, the trees,
the spirits of the ancestors
spinning in little blue orbs
that charge the bleak rocks
marked with cups and rings.

A man in deer antlers,
fox fur slung over the shoulders,
rattling a maraca of small bones,
summoning the wisdom of the ancients
fuelled by magic mushrooms.

Wet red bracken bent over
By the rain.

Politics is bullshit
Religion is a lie.
Best get drunk on vodka
And listen to the *Song of the Volga Boatmen*, baby.

The Glory of War

You can talk of the glory of war,
celebrate white headstones in rows
and the poppy red as menstrual fluid,
but I'll tell you of Archie Atkinson
a Tommy in a tin hat,
khaki uniform itching his neck,
a railway shed foreman
sent straight to the front.
with the clarts in the trench,
the stench of rotting flesh and cordite,
and how when they sent him over the top
he was hit in the ankle by machine gun fire
and toppled back into the mud
corrugated sheets and wooden slats
where an officer put his pistol to his head
until he saw the blood running free.
There's no glory in war
when they're shooting at you
from both bastard sides.

And do you know what else?
his mother-in-law
was German.

The Darkness

The bairn doesn't like the darkness;
Wants the landing light left on
And I tell him there's nowt to be scared of,
Just ask your great granddad
About the blackness doon the pit
Three miles out under the North Sea
On your hands and knees in a four foot seam
Watah running off the wahls
The crack and creak of wooden props
A helmet lamp's light glittering on the anthracite.

They send you doon in a cage
And bring you hyem in a cage.

Acknowledgements

Some of the following poems appeared in the chapbooks *Birds at Dawn* (MidNAG 1996), *Midnight at the Snake Motel* (Propaganda Press USA, 2010) and *Lucky to Get Nowt* (Blackheath Books 2011).

Thanks are due to the editors of the following where some of these poems were first published: *Acid Angel, The Beat, Clockwise Cat, Fire, Ink Sweat & Tears, Mad Swirl, Pinhole Camera, Neonbeam* and *Oasis*.